I pray anyway

DEVOTIONS FOR THE AMBIVALENT

A PLAYbook for Discussion Groups, Book Clubs, and Individual Exploration

JOYCE
WILSON-SANFORD

RED SHOE PRESS

ISBN:

978-0-9863386-1-8

Cover & Book Design:
Perch Design Studio

Foreword

Coffee is the great comforter
There in time of need
Sip—Sigh—Sip
Coffee is a connector
Come in, I'll make coffee
Coffee restores
Coffee energizes
A slurp keeps us going
Warms - holds - prepares
Accompanies tough moments of loss
Coffee stains are gorgeous, unique
Not a wrong thing
We spill
We stain
Life's a mess
A joyous mess
Come on in
Let's laugh

I PRAY ANYWAY

CONTENTS

I PRAY ANYWAY

CHAPTER ONE

CREATE YOUR OWN GAME PLAN

Playing with the Profound

After writing I PRAY ANYWAY: Devotions for the Ambivalent, I realized that the book calls for and comes alive with discussion. Each reflection is like a mini-conversation spur. I came to understand that my voice speaks for and to many people.

We are in a unique time of spiritual upheaval that is coming into clearer focus and people want to talk about it. Religion/spirituality is in turmoil today and needs fresh looks, new approaches, and grounding with what is good from the past. Many readers tell me that the reflections are probing and honest about the sensitive topic of prayer and an encouraging honest exploration of any and all things spiritual. I love the idea of "playing" with an important topic of our time rather than treating it as heavy and fraught with hotspots that lead to silence. I want to break the taboo of personal beliefs being off-limits to conversation for fear of insulting or angering or being heretical. I believe in being irreverently reverent or reverently irreverent, so—

This is a "PLAYbook" to support people creating their own exploration of the themes in *I PRAY ANYWAY*, whether alone or in a group. It is a PLAYbook, and not a WORKbook, because it is meant for enjoyment and exploration and learning (exactly why kids play).

Please approach this PLAYbook with a light heart and an open mind. In other words, play with the content. Readers can create all kinds of game plans with it and use it in many settings--which I prefer to think of as PLAYshops. A husband and wife with very different ideas (and ensuing arguments) could clarify what matters to each and why. A college class could delve into the material as a structure for a seminar. Religious leaders could use the material to hold discussions with the young adults of their membership who are evaporating at a fast rate. Brave pastors could gather a group of people who are not affiliated with any one religion to listen to their experience to understand the dynamics of the growing "non-affiliated". The PLAYbook would be perfect for a book club wanting to explore religion today. The point of any and all of this is to create good conversation, to explore ideas and gain personal insight about the immense transition that religion is going through.

Remember this is a PLAYbook, so you can pick and choose what you want to put together for your particular game plan for your particular discussion or group or PLAYshop. Play with the PLAYbook.

The simplest approach would be to start with the questions from the PLAYbook, whether from one theme or choosing a few from each chapter. Follow your own curiosity or the focus of the group using the PLAYbook. It is meant to be flexible and used for different purposes and different time constraints. A PLAYshop could range from ninety minutes to three days to once a week for several weeks.

I have included quotes that can be used to spur conversation or to begin or end a discussion or PLAYshop.

I've also included possible activities to use when a more active form of learning is wanted. You might use just one activity and one question from various PLAYbook topics for a short discussion group or you could pick and choose to custom design a PLAYshop of your own, balancing questions with activities.

I also list resources (books, blogs, magazines, videos, apps) that can add depth or background when needed to enhances the ideas in the PLAYbook.

It's impossible to give a time frame for each question or exercise because it's hard to predict what topic might "catch fire" with your group. I'm afraid you have to stay PLAYful and not over-worry that everything "gets done".

A basket of supplies is necessary for some of the experiential activities. Think PLAY box—markers, poster board, empty prayer flags to be written on, a few Nerf balls, glue, glitter—you never know what you might choose to use or what your group might choose to use. Two flip charts would be good. Think of tools and toys for playing.

Joyce Wilson Sanford

"The creation of something
new is not accomplished by the
intellect but by the play instinct."

CARL JUNG

*"Peace is not the absence of
conflict but the presence of
creative alternatives for
responding to conflict."*

DOROTHY THOMPSON

CHAPTER TWO

TALKING ACROSS DIFFERENCES

Takes Finesse

#243

Theological purity causes so many ills
Do you know
How many religious hairs can be split
In how many books
Over how many centuries?

I PRAY ANYWAY

People in the public arena don't talk much about God or religion or disbelief. People feel awkward and wary. First of all, religion and belief are very intimate subjects. I have gotten used to talking about them casually in almost any secular setting, but at the beginning of my exploration and while writing I PRAY ANYWAY, I was— embarrassed. (Now I ask strangers, "if they pray, what or who they think God is and what miracle have they recently experienced", while I'm standing in line in the grocery store.) Another reason for restraint is that no one wants to step on the powder keg of someone else's strong and opposite belief. And yet, I believe we need to talk. The people in the "middle of the muddle", as I describe them in my book, are the people who can create new approaches to the emerging modern need for the sacred.

TALKING GUIDELINES:

Before beginning your PLAYshop or conversation, I suggest acknowledging the tenderness and possible awkwardness of talking about the topic of religion/spirituality. It's good to start any discussion talking about guidelines to create comfort and candor. Start by having the group answer the following questions:

- How comfortable are you with sharing your ideas and experience about religion and spiritual life?
- What would help keep the conversation real—both safe and bold?
- Have you ever talked about the spiritual in a secular conversation with strangers?
- What are you curious about that you would like to discuss?

Ask what characteristics would make a conversation both candid and comfortable when talking about intimate, deeply held beliefs and ideas. Share a few examples to stimulate thinking and make a list of the group's responses. Be sure to include the following points:

- All voices get heard
- More asking and listening than telling or selling
- Everyone pauses to think before responding
- People ask questions to understand what someone has said, not to dispute
- Disagree with a thought, not with the person
- Periodically have one person summarize the discussion
- Anyone at any time may say, "hold it" and the discussion stops. This creates a one-minute silence break. (This break works its own kind of miracle. Feelings calm down. People think about what is happening. This one minute of silence usually clears the air and shows what direction to take next. This is not meant to be dramatic. It is a pause to recalibrate the discussion.)
- Each person asks two questions based on curiosity or to clarify a statement of another person before making a personal statement about the topic being discussed. The goal is inquiry balanced with sharing.

Next, have the group add its particular thoughts about what "kills a conversation" or discussion and how to avoid those pitfalls. Ask for a show of hands for a commitment to the norms created in discussion. Double-check whether there might be other guidelines that need to be added. Emphasize that no fake agreement is allowed. It helps to have each person give a "thumbs-up" individually to solidify their commitment.

There is one important task for an informal leader (who hopefully will still be a member of the conversation) to assure that the conversation is civil and will be stopped if it is not. If the agreed upon norms are violated it is time to stop the discussion—not as a failure but more as, "We are not ready to have this conversation right now". There is no blame assigned. The readiness is simply not there. A break is good at this time. When the break is over, a group member can summarize the commonality and differences of the conversation. There is no push or need for agreement. Never let the group end without closure especially after hitting a hotspot.

One fundamental rule is that no one has to share their thoughts or story even when asked. An easy response is "not right now". This means what it says; "No thank you, not right now". No assumption is made about the "no thank you". Participation is voluntary. Learning takes its own path.

I often end a discussion or PLAYshop with everyone shaking hands with one another and saying, "thank you". The point is a civil, warm hearted ending even if there were some slightly uncomfortable moments.

RESOURCES:

Fierce Conversations
SUSAN SCOTT

Crucial Conversations: Tools for Talking When Stakes Are High
JOSEPH GRENNY

Speaking of Faith: Why Religion Matters—and How to Talk About It
KRISTA TIPPETT

Humble Inquiry: The Gentle Art of Asking Instead of Telling
EDGAR H. SCHEIN

"Usually, when the distractions of daily life deplete our energy, the first thing we eliminate is the thing we need the most: quiet, reflective time."

SARAH BAN BREATHNACH,
SIMPLE ABUNDANCE: A DAYBOOK OF COMFORT AND JOY

CHAPTER THREE

REFLECTING ON REFLECTIONS

For Insight

#119

Yearning is a clue
My ego desires
My heart wants
My greed needs
My body craves
Only my soul yearns

I PRAY ANYWAY

This chapter title, REFLECTING ON REFLECTIONS is familiar territory for those interested in exploring religious/spiritual experience. But digging deep can begin to feel like circular thought, spinning around without being tangible. I was concerned about this issue when I decided to share my reflections. They were all very specific to me at the time I wrote them, but you as a reader don't have the backstory to each. I love hearing reactions from readers. Each reader usually has a few favorite reflections that are the ones that speak personally to them. What is interesting is when two people favor the same reflection for very different reasons and share their particular interpretation. That makes me very happy. The writing no longer belongs just to me.

QUESTIONS:

How did you use *I PRAY ANYWAY*? Did you read it in one sitting or a little each day? What worked for you?

How were the personal stories similar to your life path and how were they very different?

What were your favorite reflections? Why?

ACTIVITIES:

1. What are the themes that are embedded in the book *I PRAY ANYWAY*: Devotions for the Ambivalent? What is stimulated by the title? Create your own table of contents for the themes or ideas that emerged for you? Make them shocking or funny or bold. Make up a new title. Post the different tables of content on the wall for all to read. Note what is new and different from the original *I PRAY ANYWAY* reflections.

2. Have people note which reflection had impact or truth for them and why. People can work in pairs or groups of three to share their favorite reflections and the story they elicited.

3. In large group discussion, ask what reflection gave a negative reaction. What was it that rubbed the wrong way or that just didn't hit right? Think more about the content than the style of the reflection. Ask for those who want to share. Negative responses often generate good discussion.

4. How would you summarize the impact of the reflections? What do the reflections mean to you about God, ambivalence, prayer, the world or where you stand spiritually or religiously? Write a four-sentence reflection that captures your thoughts. This will require some time to do. Sharing is optional but is a nice way to put an ending to the topic. Have each person read their result to the group and see what emerges.

RESOURCES:

www.charterforcompassion.org

Relevant Magazine
CHRISTIAN LIFESTYLE MAGAZINE
EXPLORING THE INTERSECTION OF
FAITH AND POP CULTURE

The Lion's Roar
BUDDHIST MAGAZINE

Daily Kabbalah
GERSHON & ANDREW WEIL, M. D.

*The Art of Reflection: A Guide
to Thinking, Contemplation and
Insight on The Buddhist Path*
RATNAGUNA HENNESSEY

*"I love those who can smile
in trouble, who can gather
strength from distress, and
grow brave by reflection"*

LEONARDO DA VINCI

"We all walk a spiritual path, one that's aligned with our soul's development. Any attempt to force or manage an outcome only disrupts this alignment. As we learn to let go, we come to understand that when things don't go our way, it's because something more important to the growth of our soul is in the works."

HENRI NOUEN,
DISCERNMENT

CHAPTER FOUR

SPIRITUAL JOURNEY

Boulders and Boys

#5

I take any path
Hindu
Sufi
Christian
Jewish
I walk until a clearing opens
Then I stop
The paths go on and on
I continue

I PRAY ANYWAY

I share a kind of Cliff Notes version of my spiritual experience and growth in my book I PRAY ANYWAY: Devotions for the Ambivalent. I wanted to show the real moments and experiences that seeded my daily reflections, and to pause to look at my life from the balcony onto the dance floor, meaning to have some distance, to see patterns, and to reflect. Everyone has a story to tell about their religious/spiritual experience—or lack of it—if time is taken to look from a new perspective.

The book reflects the experience of many who want a spiritual practice or religious home base yet discover that they can't find one that fits. *I PRAY ANYWAY* shows how easy it is to sink into spiritual indifference, and that the impulse towards reverence and the sacred doesn't necessarily go away. It goes underground.

QUESTIONS:

1. Is your faith, religion or spiritual life the same as that of your parents? How is it the same? How is it different?

2. What was a high point of your spiritual life? A low point?

3. When did you experience a moment in your life that impacted your spiritual life? What was it? What happened?

4. What would you wish for the arrival at the end of your spiritual journey? Is there an "end"? What would you feel, see, understand, experience? Be as specific as possible.

ACTIVITIES:

(Assume Atheism, Humanism, etc. to be spiritual beliefs)

1. What are the eras of your spiritual/religious life? Think of them as chapters in a book and name them. Attach your ages to each chapter from birth to the present.

2. Draw a map of your spiritual journey as used in the children's game Candyland and label all of the places you've been through—Slough of Despair, Happy Dappy Island, Heartbreak Hotel, Dreamland, Steep Rocks of Reality, Roadside Rest—I could go on and on. Have fun with this. Each person shares their map and the group looks for similarities and differences in their journeys. Encourage the group to decide what is unique to each person and what looks like a historical trend.

   Questions to consider for making your map:
   - What was the state of your spiritual life during this period?
   - What religious training, if any, did you receive?
   - What relevant events occurred?

- Who were the people who most influenced your spiritual beliefs at the time?

- How did you care for your soul and spirit? What rituals did you have?

- What were your parents' attitudes toward religion or spirituality and how did they affect you?

- Who had a big impact on your view of religion?

- What event has been the most formative for your spiritual life, plus or minus?

3. Summarize your spiritual journey by creating a bumper sticker of three words.

"If you lead me astray, then my wanderings will bring me to my destination."

MICHAEL BASSEY JOHNSON

RESOURCES:

Stages of Faith
JAMES FOWLER

Man Seeks God
ERIC WEINER

A Joseph Campbell Companion
SELECTED AND EDITED BY
DIANE K. OSBON

www.spiritualityandpractice.com
RESOURCE FOR SPIRITUAL
JOURNEYS

"I have wavered between the comfortable certainty of atheism and the gnawing doubts of agnosticism my entire life."

JOHN ORTBERG

CHAPTER FIVE

AMBIVALENCE

Yes & No

#86

Right now
I am ambivalent about my ambivalence
Or sharing my ambivalence
It's tiresome
Embarrassing
Maybe cowardly
But it would be a lie to resolve it
Toward pure doubt
Or pure faith
The messy middle
Is my experience

I PRAY ANYWAY

I did use the word "ambivalent" in the title of my book, I PRAY ANYWAY: Devotions for the Ambivalent, didn't I? So, let's talk about not being able to settle in one place in regard to religious belief/spirituality.

When I started writing the book, *I PRAY ANYWAY*, I had settled for giving up any kind of prayer practice, including church or meditation. I was busy. I did feel something missing but ignored it and did just fine. Until I didn't.

As my book tells, when tragedy hit the fan, I sure remembered how to pray, which eventually led to my kind of prayer practice and the reflections in my book. I tried Atheism, which frankly, bored me. I now go to an African Methodist Episcopal church because it means business and there is lots of laughter. I swing back and forth on my position on expressing spirituality, but the arc has gotten smaller. I'm heading to living joyfully and peacefully with uncertainty.

My parents just kept it simple. They liked church. They liked potlucks. (Methodists do, you know.) They liked their fellowship. My mom once said to me, "Maybe you think too much." Maybe so.

QUESTIONS:

1. Thinking of your own religious experience, where is your ambivalence?

2. How do you handle the ambivalence?

3. The word "anyway" is important in the book title *I PRAY ANYWAY: Devotions for the Ambivalent*. What are your "anyways" when it comes to prayer? Another way is to say, "I pray even though _____"

4. Do we think too much and make faith too complicated?

ACTIVITIES:

1. Make two columns using one page of all your spiritual/religious beliefs and disbeliefs (no matter what they are). Column one is what you believe. Column two is what you do not believe.

   • What stands between these two lists that allows you to live with the personal truths on both lists?

- What title would you put at the top of both lists? How do you live with the contradictions (if any) that exist in the two lists.

- What do your lists indicate for religion and spiritually today, both for you, individually, and modern religion?

2. What would be a statement of commitment that you can honor easily that goes beyond any one religion or belief when it comes to the moral or spiritual elements of your life? Write it for yourself first. Are you willing to read it out loud? Remove anything you would not be willing to share publicly. This is a kind of personal Creed. Use the PLAYbox to create a way to honor your creed and to keep it close at hand.

RESOURCES:

Ambivalence of the Sacred: Religion, Violence and Reconciliation
R. SCOTT APPLEBY

On Ambivalence: The Problems and Pleasures of Having It Both Ways
KENNETH WEISBRODE

Devotion
DANI SHAPIRO

Faith: Essays from Believers, Agnostics and Atheists
VICTORIA ZECKHEIM

www.patheos.com
DIFFERENT PERSPECTIVES ON RELIGION AND SPIRITUALITY

"Soul never sits well with dogma."

LESLEY HAZELTON

"I enjoy believing in a God I can't define. I find this to be the most satisfactory view of God, as a force and/or source that is beyond human understanding. In fact, I see clearly now that all of the world's religions are activities in the same impulse: to give form and substance to something that is utterly above and outside our brains' ability to comprehend."

CARLTON PEARSON

CHAPTER SIX

GOD

True/False Quiz

#65

Mighty
Wow
To think of Might
Capital M might
Mighty
Powerful
Forceful
Awesome
Again, and again
I forget about the possibility of an invisible force
I am relieved
I want more than me

I PRAY ANYWAY

In Reflection #65 , I want to say that our experience of the sacred has always changed throughout history. Look at all the holy books and their continual evolution through interpretation and examination which contribute new insights as a necessity for the wisdom message to survive. Look at the Bible for an example. The Old and New Testaments are exactly that—an evolution of the experience of God-ness. All Holy Wisdom books are interpreted to preserve their essence and truth for a new generation. Does that leave us with no sure foundation? It certainly can feel that way during this chaotic time in history, but that does not mean there is no foundation.

Our spiritual evolution and maturing lead us to create new interpretation and understanding of the sacred/God-ness. Let's shift the question to, "Who is God in our world and our time? How is God experienced, and where do we find God? How is God-ness changing right now, today?"

QUESTIONS:

1. Heresy is the Greek word hairesis, which means "a choice—that is, the choice to separate or become sectioned off from the norm or tradition." What is your reaction to this definition of hairesis?

2. *I PRAY ANYWAY* hints at the idea that our modern understanding of God is changing rather than the question of "Does God exist"? How do you experience the idea (or reality) of God as changing?

3. Where do you find God-ness? More and more people are answering "not in church". So when and where do you bump into the sacred? Is it in music, nature, a new baby, a dying loved one, in silence? What brings the sacred into your life?

4. Ask yourself, is your relationship with God becoming simpler or more complicated? Or, if you have no belief in God, are you relieved or yearning?

ACTIVITIES:

1. Here are some names for God. Add a few of your own. (At one cynical stage I prayed to Dear Random Lady Luck partly as a joke and partly with some disillusionment.)

   El Olam—The Everlasting God

   Jehovah-Shalom—The Lord Our Peace

   Ar-Rahman—The Entirely Merciful

   Peleh Yo'etz—Wonderful Counselor

   El Simchatch Gili—God my exceeding joy

   Allah—The Creator, The Inventor, The Only One

   Baha—The All-Glorious

   Krishna—The Complete Supreme One In His Own Right

   Shakti—Supreme Goddess Of Dynamic Forces Moving In The Universe

   Jehovah-Raah—The Lord My Shepherd

2. What would you use as an alternate name for God that would be an accurate description for you? What name would you feel comfortable praying to/with/at?

   A fun method to inspire new names is to have people quickly shout out alternate names for God while they are captured on a flip-chart. Then have each individual vote on the most accurate and comfortable name by placing sticker dots on three of the names. Have people try a few names out loud for ease and truth until they find one that they can say comfortably.

3. What is God? Individually, have people write as many answers as they can to the question in 90 seconds. In other words, brainstorm, without thought or correction. Negative and positive answers are both good. Next create groups of three people to share their answers. In the large group ask what insights and commonalities emerged.

4. What bumper sticker about God would you be willing to put on your car? Have people put their slogan on a piece of paper and post them together on the wall without names of the authors. What do the bumper stickers say about who God is to this particular group at this particular moment?

5. What questions would you like to ask of people who have a firm belief in God? What questions would you like to ask an Atheist? What question would you like to ask an Agnostic or an Ambivalent? Depending what mix of people you have in the room, pair people with the person most different from them in faith or experience and let them ask and answer questions of one another. Take turns. Askers listen only. No discussion. Askers are gathering information, not doing anything with the differences that might emerge. Switch to a new pairing every 15 minutes. Do at least two rounds. Capture the learning.

RESOURCES:

Sacred Matters Magazine
RELIGIOUS CURRENTS IN CULTURE

Why Buddhism is True
ROBERT WRIGHT

Falling into Grace
ADYASHANTI

A Prayer Journal
FLANNERY O'CONNOR & W. A. SESSIONS

God Exists But Gawd Does Not: From Evil to New Atheism to Fine-Tuning
DAVID RAY GRIFFIN

"A mystery is not a puzzle waiting
to be solved, but rather something
for which there is no human solution.
Mystery's offspring is not frustration
but awe, and that sense of awe grows
in tandem with knowledge. The more
we know, the more we wonder."

ERIC WEINER,
MAN SEEKS GOD

"Each person is born with an unencumbered spot—free of expectation and regret, free of ambition and embarrassment, free of fear and worry—an umbilical spot of grace where we were each first touched by God. It is this spot of grace that issues peace. Psychologists call this spot the Psyche, theologians call it the Soul, Jung calls it the Seat of the Unconscious …Hindu masters call it Atman, Buddhists call it Dharma, Rilke calls it Inwardness, Sufis call it Qalb, and Jesus calls it the Center of our Love."

MARK NEPO

CHAPTER SEVEN

PRAYER

Who, What, Where, When, How

#227

I trust my own experience
Not what I'm told
Not what I read
Belief
Faith
Hope
Come from my experience
I test
And then trust
Prayer
Is my continuing experiment

I PRAY ANYWAY

Almost no one wants to talk about prayer. And yet, we do pray. According to a 2016 Pew Research Center survey, 45% of Americans and a majority of Christians (55%) say they pray daily. During tough times, many more people pray even if they describe themselves as Atheist, Agnostic or a None (non-affiliated with any religion).

That's why the word "anyway" in my book title matters so much. People have tragedy in their life and don't know where to turn. Others want something desperately. Some are adrift and feel their life has no meaning. Yet another person has a loved one who needs help. People share awe and gratitude for a spectacular blessing or miracle. And so, they pray ANYWAY. Is this praying a throwback to other times of easier belief or is prayer a stand-alone practice that needs no specific religion to undergird it?

I have been surprised by the people who tell me they don't pray because they don't know how to pray. One was the wife of a minister who said she wasn't articulate enough to pray, that she didn't have the right kind of language!!

There are really two ways to pray—borrow a prayer or create a prayer. Most, simply use the fallback prayer of their faith—the one they learned as a child. And of course, one prayer that is universal is the "God bless"—of a long list of friends and relatives (usually enemies are not included although all faiths suggest it) said before sleep.

So, how to pray? Mmmmm. It so doesn't matter. Prayer happens in so many forms. It's the truth behind the words. It's the true agony behind a moan. It's the joy in a yelp of gratitude. It's the silence that becomes full. It is the warm peace of stepping out of time for a while.

A friend of mine in San Miguel de Allende, Mexico was despondent and decided to burn some papers and letters. He tore them up into twenty plus pieces of paper. All were burned except the one phrase that was printed on the backside of a scrap of paper: "Keep prayer."

QUESTIONS:

1. Answer the who? what? when? where? how? questions (if you pray). Who do you pray to? What do you pray for? When do you pray? Where and how do you pray?

2. Have you experienced the power of prayer? Have you had a prayer answered? Share the specific story.

3. Does/can prayer stand alone, outside of formal religion?

4. When do you feel a sense of prayer when you are in the secular world with no intention of actually praying?

5. What image comes to mind when you think of praying? What does that image say to you or to others?

6. Is gratitude an automatic act of prayer?

AND A REMINDER: We are not looking for truth We are looking to share experiences and ideas. We don't need conclusions. We are opening up formerly serious, almost taboo topics for fun and exploration.

ACTIVITIES:

1. Below is a list of types of prayers. Which do you use and favor? Which do you never use?

praise	silence
gratitude	pain relief
praying for others	help
looking for guidance	listening
asking favors	

What kinds of prayers would you add? I have one that is a reflex for me. I beg about small stuff. Please, please, please find my—car keys, wallet, my calendar, that special photo, the address I'm going to. And these pleading prayers are often answered in odd and immediate ways.

2. I had a workshop participant tell me that prayer needed rebranding. If you had to sell prayer, what would you say are its benefits? What would your sales pitch be? Use twenty-five words or less. Or, what are the benefits of not praying? Either way, have people share their pitch individually with the large group or in small groups to share and discuss insights about prayer.

Another method is to have people in pairs or small groups make their case for or against prayer using ads or jingles or other marketing methods. Ask the group to vote on the most effective.

3. Have each person write a list of bold questions to ask another person about prayer, remembering that not everyone prays. (3-5 questions) Divide the group into interview pairs to ask their questions. Each person has a turn to interview and only listens to answers. After both interviews, the pairs can discuss and share insights with the whole group.

RESOURCES:

PRAYER: Does It Make Any Difference?
PHILIP YANCEY

Help, Thanks, Wow
ANNE LAMOTT

Sacred Intentions: Morning Inspirations to Strengthen the Spirit Based on the Jewish Wisdom Tradition
RABBI LORI FORMAN-JACOBI AND RABBI KERRY M. OLITZKY

Contemplative Prayer
THOMAS MERTON

The Energy of Prayer
THICH NHAT HANH

"When a doctoral student at Princeton asked, "What is there left in the world for original dissertation research?" Albert Einstein replied, "Find out about prayer. Somebody must find out about prayer."

PHILIP YANCEY,
PRAYER

"Bertrand Russell was asked what will you do if, after you die, it turns out that God exists? What will you do if you come face-to-face with this God whom you've defied your whole life long?" Bertrand Russell responded that he would point his finger at God and say, "You, sir, gave us insufficient evidence."

JOHN ORTBERG,
FAITH AND DOUBT

CHAPTER EIGHT

FAITH AND DOUBT
Learning to Live Together

#17

So many people thinking they are right
Knowing truth about mystery
Trying to lock it down their way
Mystery won't have it
So why not just
Know the 'not knowing'
Be sure of that

I PRAY ANYWAY

And now let's tackle this topic—belief or not so much belief. We live in a polarized world. There are those who really, really, really believe and those who really, really, really don't.

To many of us, either extreme seems—well, extreme. Many of us now hang out in what I call "the middle of the muddle" where nothing quite fits fully when it comes to our spiritual lives. We are in a historic moment in which more and more people don't share an unquestioned common belief. We are in a spiritual free fall until new forms and approaches are created that ground us—that satisfy our brains, our hearts and our souls. Until that happens (and it is happening) we are left hanging. Certitude even feels dangerous as we see the violence that comes from clashing "rightness". How do we live in "the in between time" needed to refresh and renew all religions and mature our spiritual lives? Here are my answers:

- We live with patience and forbearance.
- We trust our own experience.
- We mind our mouths.
- We are gracious under attack but not weak.
- We remember we are in transition as a world.
- We wait for clarity that lasts.
- We celebrate the courage of walking with an unclear path.
- We realize we are all spiritual explorers as the beliefs of the world go through a new winnowing to find common sacred space.

QUESTIONS:

1. Discuss the answers given above. Add yours.

2. If you were to substitute different words for "faith" and "doubt", what would they be?

3. Who is a strong doubter that you admire? And who is a strong believer that you admire? What lessons do both teach you?

4. What is the good part about doubt and the bad part about faith?

ACTIVITIES:

1. Use the continuum that follows to support discussion about faith and doubt. (Duplicate the continuum on a poster board or flip chart and ask people to mark where they stand by placing a dot sticker on the continuum. Invite people to explain where and why they "stand" on the continuum.

UNSHAKEABLE FAITH ——————————— FULL DOUBT

2. What is your personal stumbling block about moving more toward Faith or toward Doubt? Do you want to move in either direction? This could be a good time to do something creative and concrete. Using the PLAYbox, have people create a literal stumbling block out of materials in the box. Each person would present their stumbling block. This could also be done more simply with each person making an image of their stumbling block. Ask each individual how they handle their stumbling block.

3. Have participants divide a large paper in half to make two columns. Label one side "What I know" and the other side "What I don't know" They are to fill in both columns answering this question,"When I think about religion, spiritual life, and the sacred, here is what I know and don't know". Post this work on a wall so everyone can wander and read what people have written. Then have each person go to their columns to add a conclusion by finishing this sentence: "And so—." As, always share insights and learning.

RESOURCES:

www.beliefnet.org

Faith
KRISTA TIPPETT

www.patheos.com,
THE FRIENDLY ATHEIST

Letters from a Skeptic
DR. GREGORY BOYD

Why Science Does Not Disprove God
AMIR ACZEL

"Sometimes I think it is my mission to bring faith to the faithless, and doubt to the faithful."

PAUL TILLICH

"The human ego, in contrast to the divine ego, is self-centered, boastful, and focused only on self-gratification. The divine ego is about profound gratitude, knowledge of self as eternal, and the desire to manifest God's creative glory for all. It is a generous spirit of creation, not hoarding or self-aggrandizing."

PAUL TILLICH

CHAPTER NINE

THE EGO DILEMMA

Too big, Too little, Just right

#288

I am embarrassed
By what my ego gets me into
When it deflates
I am chagrined
By the ego hangover
I have to live with
Thank goodness for humor

I PRAY ANYWAY

Like many people on a spiritual journey, I'm continually wrestling with my ego. I want to grow, but often it's ego that trips me up. Spiritual and psychological development experts say that, of course you have to develop a strong ego—in order to let it go. Inflated egos are puffed up and grandiose. Deflated egos are weak and quickly turn into being easily taken advantage of, or victimized. The middle ground ego is strong, able to be generous, loses nothing by giving and knows how to protect itself. A strong ego can let go and shift to humility without loss of self. Many of the reflections in I PRAY ANYWAY laugh at my sudden realization of my inflated ego. Getting to know your ego and how to manage it has a strong spiritual component.

QUESTIONS:

1. Who are famous people (dead or alive) who are examples of an inflated ego, a deflated ego and a strong and healthy ego? What are the qualities of each person?

2. What are moments in your life where your ego is not strong enough? What are moments when you are too full of yourself? When is your ego just right, and what does that feel like?

3. How do you move from deflated ego or inflated ego to healthy ego? What techniques do you use?

"I remembered reading the account of a spiritual seeker who interrupted a busy life to spend a few days in a monastery praying. "I hope your stay is a blessed one," said the monk who showed the visitor to his cell. If you need anything, let us know and we'll teach you how to live without it."

PAUL TILLICH

ACTIVITIES:

1. Seat the group in a circle. Ask each person to write a description of a present ego dilemma they are experiencing on a full sheet of paper. When finished have each person pass the paper to the person on their left. Each recipient writes a one sentence solution to the dilemma on the front side of the paper. Pass the paper for comments to at least three people.

    Return the dilemma to each original writer to read the solutions offered for their ego dilemma. Have people share insights from the comments they received with the group as a whole.

2. If you were to surrender your ego and accept your life just as you are and just as your life is, what would you have to let go of? Write a letter to yourself about what you would have to surrender. Be specific. There is power in private time to think and write, so allow time for this exercise. Ask for volunteers to share insights that came through the writing.

3. What words of acceptance would calm your human ego and allow you to shift to the universal ego of gratitude and generosity? Write a blessing to your ego to allow this shift. Create a way to carry this blessing with you using the PLAYbox materials. Depending on the environment and time allotted, these blessings could be read aloud by the person or by a group member. They could also be put on a wall for viewing to show that ego struggles tend to be very similar.

RESOURCES

www.lionsroar.com
BUDDHIST WISDOM FOR OUR TIME

The Gift of Imperfection
BRENE BROWN

Archetypes
CAROLYN MYSS

The Shadow Effect: Illuminating the Hidden Power of Your True Self
DEEPAK CHOPRA, MARIANNE WILLIAMSON AND DEBBIE FORD

"How do I regain my wonder at being alive? What must I do to keep my heart from sinking?"

MARK NEPO,
THE BOOK OF AWAKENING

CHAPTER TEN

HARD TIMES

Can't We Do Without Them?

#211

A book title I remember
Suffering Is Optional
Clever
Not true
Suffering just is
Buddhists cool it way down
Neutralize it
Christians tend to fall in love with it
Sufis chase it away with ecstasy
Others affirm it away with positive thinking
I turn it to sorrow
And then sorrow to sweetness
An alchemy of sorts

I PRAY ANYWAY

Hard times. My assumption is everyone has hard times. Sometimes I see people whose life seems to run smoothly—until I get to know them better.

I have an inner novelist or story teller that comes out when I am talking with someone and I can't resist making my hard times somewhat funny when I tell them. They are the stuff of my life, and there is lots of absurdity and randomness and incredibly odd incidents in my troubles and pain. Every once in a while, I see the face of someone listening to me cringe with shock or hurt for me. Then I know that their hard times have been different from mine. At other times, my partner in conversation joins me in a good laugh. Then, I know our hard times were similar.

I have crawled through some doozies and have learned when to give a cosmic shrug at what just can't be understood with a close-up lens. The spiritual lens gives distance and meaning and personal deepening to those absolutely lousy, even tragic hard times. We literally live and learn.

QUESTIONS:

1. Count the unmistakably hard times in your life, those that have been life changers, that demanded a new response from you. How many have you had? Now count the unmistakably wonderful events in your life that have been life changers that created a new response from you. Share the number in both categories and share any insights from your thoughts with the group. Did you learn equally from hard times and good times? Were the lessons similar?

2. Think of a specific hard time; how did you live through it? What tools and techniques could you share that might help others?

3. We live in a hard time in our world. How are you impacted? What helps you? What helps the world?

4. How do you build relief and moments of respite into a hard time? In other words, how do you care for yourself when you are in a gut-wrenching excruciating time in your life?

ACTIVITIES:

1. Ask individuals to describe a hard time they are in presently by writing five specific elements of the situation. Next have them partner with another person whose job it is to write the opposite of the specific elements of the hard time. Then together talk about how to build a bridge from the elements of the hard time to the elements of the good time. Each person in the pair does the activity. Building this transitional bridge is essential to moving forward.

2. Design a symbol or depict a hard time that you are experiencing. For example, someone wanting to lose weight could show an open mouth crammed with food. Next, put people in groups of three to help one another design a symbol or depiction of a counter attack on the hard time. Use the PLAYbox. For instance, someone could put a fence over the open mouth crammed with food. Or make the food ugly. This is the gift of working playfully with other people. New insights come in an interesting way.

3. Write a thank you note to the most impactful hard time of your life. What is your reaction to writing this note? Decide what you want to do with the note. Destroy it or display it?

RESOURCES:

Transitions: Making Sense of Life's Changes
WILLIAM BRIDGES

When Bad Things Happen to Good People
HAROLD S. KUSHNER

When Things Fall Apart: Heart Advice for Difficult Times
PEMA CHODRON

The Book of Joy
DALAI LAMA AND DESMOND TUTU WITH DOUGLAS ABRAMS

Gratitude
OLIVER SACHS

"Life has bold intentions, lazy happenstances, and unintended consequences, yet I also believe that there are connections that illuminate our world, revealing its endless mystery and wonder"

DAVID MARANISS

CHAPTER ELEVEN

MIRACLES
Get No Respect

#2

Let great big wonderful things be possible
Let's quit dumbing down our hope
Why not why not why not wonderful?
Step me into free fall
Take my breath away
Let's have marvels
Miracles
We are at that point
The impossible is mandatory

I PRAY ANYWAY

miracle |ˈmirək(ə)l| *noun*
*a surprising and welcome event that is not explicable by natural
or scientific laws and is therefore considered to be the work of
a divine agency*
NEW OXFORD AMERICAN DICTIONARY

*I have experienced big fat miracles in my life and many daily mini-
miracles. I do marvel and tell their story and am grateful beyond
belief for my miracles. "Beyond belief" is right. I don't believe in
miracles, but they happen. And mine are usually "prayed for"—*

praying "anyway"—with and without belief. I have been healed of a lump in my breast. I have had money come my way in the exact amount needed. I have found lots of lost items (not the usual absentminded kind) when I am desperate for them. In fact, I tend to test God-ness with finding the lost article. In the back of my head, I say, "Prove yourself God". And when I find the lost article, I immediately say, "That was lucky". That last sentence shows exactly what I mean about how we disregard miracles—writing them off as luck. Let's talk miracles.

QUESTIONS:

1. Have you ever experienced what you would call a miracle? What made it a miracle?

2. How is a miracle different from "good luck"?

3. Where does a miracle come from? Does it have to be from God? If not, what is the alternative?

ACTIVITIES:

1. Let's look at big, wonderful, mysterious miracles. Have people share a major miracle with another person in the group. They're usually accompanied by awe and gratitude. Share a major miracle you have experienced with another person in the group, Do not hurry this conversation. Set a time limit as a guide, but let people wallow in these wonderful happenings. Groups of three would be better for a large group. The task is to jointly create a report to the larger group entitled, Insights on Miracles. Use the questions that follow:

- What do these large miracles have in common?
- What were the feelings and actions taken before the miracle?
- What did you tell yourself about the miracle afterward?
- How and why do you think it came about?

2. Miracles happen. They exist. Lives have been saved. Symbols of loved ones who have died appear. Unexpected grace gives you exactly what you want with no effort on your part. In the Mexican culture, people make a memorial of a miracle by painting a representation of the event as a thank you note to the sacred. The drawings are very primitive and simple. Make a memorial for your major miracle. Post them around the room for all to enjoy and discuss. Keep the memorial as a memento of your gratitude.

3. How do miracles come about? Write a letter to an imaginary eight-year-old, explaining what a miracle is and how they happen. Share these and enjoy the variety of explanations. Even better, ask an eight-year-old how miracles happen.

RESOURCES:

Mind Yoga,
FRANCES SCOVEL SHINN

Outrageous Openess
TOSHA SILVER

Daily Kaballah
GERSHON WINKLER AND
ANDREW WEIL, M.D.

The Spontaneous Attainment of Desire
DEEPAK CHOPRA

The Biology of Belief: Unleashing the Power of Consciousness
BRUCE H. LIPTON

"As we enter the path of transformation, the most valuable thing we have working in our favor is our yearning."

CYNTHIA BOURGEAULT,
THE WISDOM JESUS:
TRANSFORMING HEART AND MIND

CHAPTER TWELVE

YEARNING

The Cosmic Itch

#307

Not everyone has this itch
This irritation
This curiosity
This lonely ache
This 'nothing's right'
In the middle of a really good life
That prompts a search
For the divine
Lucky me

I PRAY ANYWAY

There are plenty of things in my life that I don't like or want to change. They are normal life irritations. My life has enough joy and richness and abundance in it that the heavier moments in my life are outweighed by the good. Certainly, I am impacted by the external world with its many challenges.

However, even in the best times for me and the world, I have an edge of discontent that floats above my head. It feels like homesickness or a thought I want to shake off or a yearning without knowing for what.

It is a kind of spiritual crankiness or cosmic itch. I am not pathological. I am human. Humans yearn. It seems we have an inborn instinct or urge to connect with the divine. As Jane Fonda at age seventy said, "I had a sudden urge for reverence."

QUESTIONS:

1. Do you experience a kind of spiritual blues that doesn't make sense to you? If you do, what is it like? When does it hit you? How do you handle it? How strong is your "cosmic" itch?

2. How does our world/culture support this yearning or instinct, and how does it mute or prevent it?

3. Where do you talk about this unscratched itch? Do you talk about it at all? Who do you talk to about it?

4. How does formal religion or worship impact this yearning? Does it?

ACTIVITIES:

1. Give each person a sheet of paper with a vertical line dividing it. On the left side, ask participants to list those things that support spiritual searching. On the right, ask that they list those things that don't. Which side has the most influence? Ask people to title the paper and post it on the wall with the others of the group. Give time for reading each posting. What do the results say about the spiritual aspect in our present culture?

2. How is it possible to differentiate everyday discontent from the "cosmic itch"? Put people in pairs to make criteria for what is secular discontent and irritation and what is a spiritual discontent and irritation. Share results with the whole group to look for commonalities and differences.

3. We live in a time of epidemic suicide. Federal data shows that

suicide rates have been increasing for years in almost every state in the US. Is there a spiritual component to suicide beyond mental health, highly individual circumstances and socio-economic factors? How could it be recognized? Make groups of 4 or five and ask that they create guidelines for the prevention of suicide from spiritual despair. They must make their own definitions of words and concepts they use. Each group will report out.

RESOURCES:

Waiting for God
ANDREW MURRAY

The Seat of the Soul
GARY ZUKAV

Modern Man (and woman-my addition) in Search of a Soul
C. G. JUNG AND W. S. DELL

Entering the Castle: Finding the Inner Path to God and Your Soul's Purpose
CAROLINE MYSS

"Humans are wired to seek a god or gods."

MARGARET ATWOOD

"Let me seek, then, the gift of silence, and poverty, and solitude, where everything I touch is turned into a prayer: where the sky is my prayer, the birds are my prayer, the wind in the trees is my prayer, for God is all in all."

THOMAS MERTON,
THOUGHTS IN SOLITUDE

CHAPTER THIRTEEN

SOLITUDE AND SILENCE

The Sacred Hush

#73

Joy is there waiting
In the silence
And solitude
My cup of coffee hot
My cup of hope
My everyday chalice

I PRAY ANYWAY

Just the words, solitude and silence, soothe and fill me. I had very little of either in my early adult life except for reading in bed five minutes before snoring. I had a great solitude/activity balance as a child. I was never lonely. I lived in a blue-collar neighborhood and my block had thirty-five kids ready to play. I just stepped into the street when I wanted playmates.

But I also had my own private space that was equally rich and compelling to me. There was a bridal wreath bush in my backyard that had far-reaching, droopy branches that I could sit under and, well, just sit. I had a small card table in the living room that I would cover with a sheet and sit under and, well, just sit. I had a space between my garage and the neighbor's with a big lilac bush at one end. I could hide there too and, well, just sit. Even as I describe them now, I can see the details of each location. The wire fence behind the bridal wreath, the rusty legs of the card table, and the peeling brown paint of the neighbor's garage stay in my memory exactly as I saw them then, vivid and particular.

Then childhood turned into a running-pace life. Not until I was fifty-years-old, did I experience that kind of disappearing from the worldness that I had as a child. The next time I felt that same recollection of self and magic was when my very large family was gone all at the same time for a week. I was fifty years old! I couldn't re-gather the pieces of myself fast enough. It was winter and there was a blizzard. Everything had to hold still. I was giddy with the freedom. Don't picture meditation. I ate a bag of Snickers Bars leftover from Halloween. I wore only pajamas. Eventually I settled down from the giddiness of freedom and sat in front of a fire in the fireplace every morning and every evening. I wrote about it in a tiny book I called SOLITUDE LOG—both burning a log and keeping a log. I've been addicted, ever since, to solitude and silence.

QUESTIONS:

1. Where was your childhood alone space? Describe it and how you used it.

2. Are you a solitude and silence avoider or addict?

3. If and when you are in extended silence and solitude, what happens? What stages do you go through?

4. What balance of silence/solitude do you want in your life? Do you consider both essential?

ACTIVITIES:

1. Where is your refuge? Design the perfect space for you to recover your sense of self and awe in your life. What five things would have to be in it? Ask people to make a collage or blueprint of their refuge. Post the results and note the very individual results.

2. List all the activities of a normal week. Divide those activities into a pie chart or put a percentage of time spent for each activity over the one-week period. Would you trade any activity for time alone? How would you make this happen? Create groups of three people to share their results and reactions.

3. Have participants try to sell the benefits of solitude and silence to a reluctant customer played by another participant. Encourage the conversation to be real, not a role play. Share results in the larger group. This could be done in front of the group followed by discussion or in smaller groups with two members demonstrating the conversation of promoting and resisting the benefits of solitude.

RESOURCES:

Dialogues with Silence
THOMAS MERTON

Journey to the Heart: Christian Contemplation Through the Centuries
KIM NATARAJA

The Way of the Heart: Connecting with God Through Prayer Wisdom, and Silence
HENRI J.M. NOUEN

Silence: The Mystery of Wholeness
ROBERT SARDELLO AND THERESE SCHROEDER-SHEKER

"When peace, like a river, attendeth my way,
When sorrows like sea billows roll,
Whatever my lot, Thou has taught me to say
It is well, it is will with my soul"

HORATIO SPOFFARD

CHAPTER FOURTEEN

SOUL

Winner of the Spiritual Games

#234

Of course I can be happy
With my soul out of whack
I love my bling
My grandkids
My porch
Popcorn
All life's goodies
But who wants to be only happy

I PRAY ANYWAY

I am interested in "soul" for several reasons. One is because it is the least discordant topic in any of the conversations I've had with participants in the PLAYshops I've held. When we talk about modern religion, close to eighty-percent of the people in my PLAYshops believe in the existence of soul, almost as a matter of fact. There is not much argument about the reality or the experience of the soul. On the other hand, when talking about God or faith or a higher power, many people get slightly testy, or uneasy, at the difference of opinions in the room.

Miracles are enjoyed but shrugged off when it comes to their origination. Miracles are like awesome answers on steroids. They come. They are magnificent. They go. They recede into luck or coincidence.

Soul on the other hand stays steady. Some say it resides somewhere in or around the person. It can be seen as a guardian that squawks when we go in the wrong direction. Or it can be seen as a tutor giving life lessons for people to discover their life purpose. For others, it's a resting place, a restoration station that re-calibrates how to live in the world.

For many it is a spiritual essence of who they are that will remain vital and active after the death of the body. The living after death of the soul gets a high degree of acceptance without answering the big metaphysical questions, such as how does a soul remain after bodily death, where does it hang out waiting for the next incarnation and what is its relationship to personality? Let's talk about soul.

QUESTIONS:

1. Think of your soul as a person (play with the concept and don't worry about what is "true"). Name him or her. Describe your soul's attributes.

2. When do you feel the presence of your soul? Where are you when you experience your soul? What is going on? What are you doing? What does the awareness of your soul feel like when you are most soul aware? If you don't accept soul as "real", what is your experience when others talk about soul. What is your equivalent? Is there an equivalent?

3. When do you experience soul in others? What is it that makes a person or a situation feel "soulful"?

ACTIVITIES:

1. Break the group into subgroups of 2-4 people, depending on the size of the group. Give each group 5-10 minutes to define soul in concrete terms. Next, have the original subgroups join another subgroup to continue work on a definition of soul that they can all agree on. Allow 20 minutes. There must be agreement on the definition for soul. The disagreed upon elements can be put into a list of "leftover" elements. The task is to push for an agreed upon definition of soul for the group with as few leftover elements as possible. This will take time and need a leader to help refine the agreed upon elements as well as the leftovers that don't have high agreement. Discuss insights and conclusions from the work.

2. Ask each person to find a spot to sit with enough space to feel removed from others. The task is for each person to listen for their soul or inner voice. Allow 15 minutes of quiet. If needed, play music, but very softly. At the end of the fifteen minutes ask the following questions for the individuals to consider and write down:

- What does your soul want you to do?

- What might you be afraid of gaining?

- If you were to fully honor your soul priorities, what would you be afraid of losing?

- What is your soul prompting you to do?

Ask People to share what the experience was like. They can share the promptings of their soul or inner voice if they volunteer. Make sure to allow for negative experiences.

3. There are two quotes in this chapter that talk about the well-being of a soul. One says, "Thus sings my soul". And the other says, "It is well, it is well, with my soul".

Ask each person write to a list of what makes their soul or inner voice sing and makes it well. Next have each individual write a list of what kills the song of their soul and makes it very unwell. Ask people to join another to share their lists. The next task is to support one another to make a health plan for his or her soul. The mandate is how to do more of what feeds the soul and less of what starves it. A simple format can be used such as a Do More/ Do Less list. In the large group, discuss reactions to the activity.

RESOURCES:

The Untethered Soul: The Journey Beyond Yourself
MICHAEL SINGER

Soul Keeping: Caring for the Most Important Part of You
JOHN ORTBERG

www.soulcare.com

"One of the main differences in the new personal religion is going deep rather than being right. This means studying your tradition or others that attract you and following them in your own sincere way and wholeheartedly."

THOMAS MOORE,
A RELIGION OF ONE'S OWN

CHAPTER FIFTEEN
SPIRITUAL PIONEERING
No Gear Required

#19

I am known for a kind of joy
Nothing makes me happier than a rule well broken
Just a little naughtiness makes my day
And so, I don't act my age
Mainly because I don't know it
But I've decided to let myself get older
More deep peace
More forgiveness
More letting go of achievement
More noodling on the miracles
But I will always dance in the kitchen
And break a rule that needs it

I PRAY ANYWAY

Pioneer | ˌpīəˈnir | noun
a person who is among the first to research and develop a new area of
knowledge or activity

NEW OXFORD AMERICAN DICTIONARY

We are living in a major transitional period in history. Understanding this fact can help with the sense of chaos, helplessness and anxiety that we live in daily. The search for happiness is like a virus and has become a commodity to sell as a cure. As the number of people leaving formal religions grows, we find ourselves rudderless, looking for direction and a moral compass to get us through this historical passage.

We need pioneers of all kinds to explore and find new paths to create harmonious ways to live together on this planet. We are in need of a new spiritual fitness to support our aspirations for a different, kinder world. We need a spiritual personal practice of our own making, perhaps relying, on much of our traditional belief, but with more richness, everyday-ness and depth. New forms will appear for differently organized religion. This pioneering is happening right now. Love, compassion and empathy, are beginning to be taught as practical skills in the world. We are all pioneers whether we know it or not.

QUESTIONS:

1. What attracts you about being a spiritual pioneer? What don't you like about the idea?

2. If you were to be a spiritual pioneer what would be different in your life?

3. What do you see in our world and time that indicates that spiritual pioneers are needed?

4. What parts of your religious tradition or Atheism (which is its own belief) would you get rid of? What would you keep and cherish? What would you create?

ACTIVITIES:

1. Ask each person to invent a "liturgical/spiritual practice" calendar for the year, marking dates that would make a cycle of reverence and gratitude and worship. This could include setting aside time for

personal retreat or spiritual nourishment. The calendar is to be used to remind that spiritual fitness takes effort. Before individuals start to create their "liturgical calendar" ask the group as a whole to throw out ideas to stimulate creativity. Use the PLAYbox materials to make the calendars practical and usable.

2. Have a conversation with the group as a whole about the characteristics and qualities of a pioneer? Don't discuss as they toss out the ideas. After the list is completed, discuss how these qualities relate to being a "spiritual" pioneer. What does being a "spiritual" pioneer look like? Why be one? Why not? Do people well- grounded in their particular faith need to be pioneers?

3. Decide what your spiritual pioneering could look like. Next draw three footprints on a piece of paper. (The blank footprints could be provided.) The footprints are leading you into your spiritual exploration. Write on each footprint the steps that you need and want to take. Trade the footprints with another person in the group. Ask that person to add a fourth footprint to make you a bolder pioneer, to add a new aspect. Share reactions to the exercise. Discuss the role of commitment to pioneering. What pioneering tools are needed?

RESOURCES:

Holistic Islam: Sufism, Transformation, and The Needs of Our Time
KABIR HELMINSKI

Choosing Our Religion: The Spiritual Lives of America's Nones
ELIZABETH DRESCHER

Fingerprints of God: What science is Learning About the Brain and Spiritual Experience
BARBARA BRADLEY HAGGERTY

Einstein's God: Conversations About Science and the Human Spirit
KRISTA TIPPET

The Religion of Tomorrow: A Vision for the Future of the Great Traditions-More Inclusive, More Comprehensive, More Complete
KEN WILBER

"I am the dance, and the dance goes on
Dance, dance, wherever you may be
I am the lord of the dance, said he
And I lead you all, wherever you may be
And I lead you all in the dance, said he"

METHODIST HYMNAL 261

CHAPTER SIXTEEN
END STATEMENT
So What?

#250

I believe that something good could happen
Is happening
All acts of good count
All moments of gratitude lift everyone
All stretching to get to love strengthens us
All awareness of Now wakes us
All prayers add to the mix
Of something good happening

I PRAY ANYWAY

So what? After talking and thinking and playing reverently and irreverently about all things spiritual and religious, so what? This was often the most important question I used in meetings with my colleagues at work. It's just blunt enough to bring out meaning after floundering or creating together (often both the same thing) and to tie-up loose ends.

Answering "so what?" tells you where you stand after being open to differences. It allows you to digest an experience and to incorporate what you want and to expel the rest. Why bother with exploring if you can't answer "so what" as a result?

Here is my "so what" from my spiritual work and exploration up to this point to use as examples. They are continuing to change and emerge.

- Prayer is good for me. It makes me more content, no matter what goes on in my life, and rejuvenates my energy and optimism.

- I believe in God-ness. I have experienced it as inexplicable guidance and a source of love and creativity.

- I like standing in the middle. I don't want hard and fast resolution to my questions. The middle is the right place for me to stand right now.

- Hard times just are.

- Miracles are underrated.

- Mystery intrigues me.

- Silence and solitude are my home.

- I want to know more about Quantum Physics and its relationship to spiritual growth in the coming together of science and religion.

- I am glad for the "cosmic itch" that leads me to a new richness and depth in the spiritual element of my life.

QUESTIONS:

1. What learning, ideas, or feelings stick with you at the end of your time playing with the ideas in the I PRAY ANYWAY PLAYbook, either as an individual or as a member of a PLAY group?

2. What are you curious to explore further?

3. What do you know now that you didn't before exploring with the PLAYBOOK?

4. How do you answer, "So what?"

ACTIVITIES:

NOTE: It is best to take care of any logistics or practical follow-up before beginning the following closing activities. Start this work with the definition of a blessing that follows:

Blessing | 'blesiNG | noun
a beneficial thing for which one is grateful; something that brings well-being or favor or protection from God. Blessings can be given person to person and not only from a formal religious role.
NEW OXFORD AMERICAN DICTIONARY

1. Ask each person to write a blessing for her or himself, wishing good things for life. Encourage the use of the PLAYbox materials to add a touch of beauty or whimsy. The group will form a circle and each person will pass their self- blessing to the person on their right. That person will read out loud the blessing for the person who wrote it. No discussion needed until all the blessings have been read.

   Then have the group discuss what it felt like to be blessed out loud by another person with the exact right blessing wanted and needed? How could blessings be used in a more everyday way?

2. To end the PLAYshop, create groups of two or three to create a blessing for the work and the play that the group has done together. Have each subgroup read the blessing to the group. Allow for some silence before breaking the group by handshakes all round. The PLAYshop is over.

RESOURCES:

Blessings
JOHN O'DONAHUE

www.beliefnet.org

www.thehumanist.org

www.charterforcompassion.org

Enlightenment Now
STEVEN PINKER

"The thing to do, it seems to me, is to prepare yourself so you can be a rainbow in somebody else's cloud. Somebody who may not look like you. May not call God the same name you call God—if they call God at all. I may not dance your dances or speak your language. But be a blessing to somebody. That's what I think."

MAYA ANGELOU

I PRAY ANYWAY

AFTERWORD

COME EXPLORE WITH ME

Come play in the sandbox of spiritual ideas and personal development.

This book will never be finished.
It needs your voice and contributions.

PLEASE SEND ME:

- **Resources** that support and provoke spiritual development
- **Additional themes** that are needed in the PLAYbook
- **New activities** and questions or refinements to those already in the PLAYbook
- **Ideas** on how this companion book to *I PRAY ANYWAY* can be used.

CONTACT JOYCE
joycewilsonsanford@gmail.com
or *readjoyce.com*

HIRE JOYCE
Training for use of the Playbook

Individual Spiritual Development Coaching

PURCHASE BOOKS
at *Amazon.com*
and at *readjoyce.com*

CONNECT
Facebook: @IPrayAnyway

I PRAY ANYWAY

.

ABOUT THE AUTHOR

Joyce Wilson-Sanford is a former Executive Vice President for a global company, The Delhaize Group. She now works as an executive coach and is the writer of three unique and diverse blogs, I Pray Anyway, CEO Note to Self, and Truth Burps which can be found at joycewilsonsanford.com. She has been a frequent keynote speaker and leader of workshops on innovation, leadership development, and large system change. Now, she turns to writing with the same energy and commitment that she brings to her professional work.

Joyce's work and point of view is global. Three years in the Peace Corps profoundly shifted her into being a world citizen. Her work as a global executive took her to Belgium, Greece, The Czech Republic, Romania, Thailand and Indonesia. Now, Joyce and her husband live and work from Maine, splitting their time with Mexico.

Joyce's life has had its share of profound challenges and she has gone through many permutations of devotional practices including having none. She has lived the modern woman's life from stay at home mom to divorced single parent to step family working mom to Senior Executive. She and her second husband raised five children and worked more than full time. From the bumps and bruises of her life, she has emerged with a very real, engaging wisdom that she shares in this book. Joyce speaks the language of the spiritually independent and articulates the ambivalence of the growing group who are religiously disenfranchised. She brings a unique voice to all her endeavors and insists that life and work have meaning and spiritual depth (which automatically means fun and humor) in an easy and natural way.

I PRAY ANYWAY

ACKNOWLEDGEMENTS

Finishing this book has been an act of perseverance.
Living a life took precedence time and time again.
Thanks to the following who hung in there with me:

Ariette Scott
creative consultant, editor and
colleague

Judy Gagnon
my needed creative and boldness
support for the pilot of the PLAYshop

Meghan Lambert
for book and cover design for
ultimate patience and flexibility

Katherine Cauley & Pat Newcomb
early supporters in all kinds of
ways—and they buy books

Eileen Kalikow
for her tough "schoolmarm"
proofreading accompanied by wine
and welcome

Carol Eleazer
my Guardian Angel who spurs me
on with ideas & support at just the
right time

Dr. Anthony McCann
who kept his interest in this book
when I lost mine

And big thanks to the Beta PLAYshop members who came with curiosity
and took the PLAYshop from idea into a concrete product.

Rabbi Gary Berenson
Andrew Bracy
Steve Brinn
Peter Hayes
Susan Howe
Joshua Hughes
Eileen Kalikow

Amey Leadley
Jean Ginn Marvin
Colby Marvin
Tony McCann
Lisa Miller
Bob Ray